BONE MAP

BONE MAP

poems | SARA ELIZA JOHNSON

MILKWEED EDITIONS

Published 2014 by Milkweed Editions
Printed in the United States of America
Cover design by Mary Austin Speaker
Author photo by Fotofly Studio
19 20 21 22 23 6 5 4 3 2
First Edition

Milkweed Editions, an independent nonprofit publisher, gratefully acknowledges sustaining
support from the Bush Foundation; the Jerome Foundation; the Lindquist & Vennum Foundation;
the McKnight Foundation; the National Endowment for the Arts; the Target Foundation; and other
generous contributions from foundations, corporations, and individuals. Also, this activity is made
possible by the voters of Minnesota through a Minnesota State Arts Board Operating Support grant,
thanks to a legislative appropriation from the arts and cultural heritage fund, and a grant from the
Wells Fargo Foundation Minnesota. For a full listing of Milkweed Editions supporters, please visit
milkweed.org.

Library of Congress Cataloging-in-Publication Data
Johnson, Sara Eliza.
 [Poems. Selections]
 Bone Map : poems / Sara Eliza Johnson. -- First edition.
   pages cm. -- (National Poetry Series)
 ISBN 978-1-57131-469-7 (alk. paper) -- ISBN 978-1-57131-919-7 (ebook)
 I. Title.
 PS3610.O3764A6 2014
 811'.6--dc23
                          2014004616

CONTENTS

Fable   *3*

Deer Rub   *4*

Beekeeping   *6*

As the Sickle Moon Guts a Cloud   *8*

Märchen   *9*

Lesson   *11*

Me Tangere   *12*

Rapture   *13*

View From the Fence, On Which I Sit and Dangle My Legs   *15*

Confession   *17*

Frühlingstraum   *18*

The Last Przewalski's Horse   *19*

The Dream of Water   *21*

Parable of the Flood   *22*

When There Is Burning Instead   *23*

Purgatory   *25*

Epilogue   *26*

———

Pathfinder   *30*

———

Sea Psalm   *36*

Question   *37*

Elegy Surrounded by Water   *38*

Archipelago: Island of Sheep   *40*

Archipelago: The Paradise of Birds   *42*

Archipelago: Tabula Rasa   *43*

Archipelago: The Soporific Well   *45*

Instructions for Wintering on the Ice Field   *46*

Letter from the Ice Field, October   *47*

Letter from the Ice Field, December   *48*

Letter from the Ice Field, January   *50*

Letter from the Ice Field, March   *51*

Archipelago: Ultima Thule   *53*

The City Where Men Are Mended   *55*

Let Us Consider Where We Might Have a Home   *57*

How the World Was Made   *59*

Equinox   *60*

A god steps down from the mountain. He walks through the dark forest. There are wild beasts everywhere in the silent darkness. It must be real. I'm not dreaming. I'm telling the truth.

INGMAR BERGMAN
Through a Glass Darkly

BONE MAP

Fable

In the forest, the owl releases a boneless cry.
I know the names of things here
and I can hold them.
I hold your hand:
a matryoshka opening deeper
until I can hear your bones
singing into mine,
and feel the moon

as it rolls through you
like a great city before a war
where it has been night for so long
that everyone sees
with their hands,
and then somewhere in the city
a newborn animal
shakes the dust off itself

and stands, makes
a thimbleful of sound,
and a boy standing in the square
turns toward it,
and his father, not knowing
what his hands will be made to do
to other men,
places a hand on his head.

Deer Rub

Deep in the forest, where no one has gone,
where rain bloats the black moss and mud,

a deer is rubbing its forelock and antlers
against a tree. The velvet that covers the antlers

unwinds into strips, like bandages.
The rain scratches at the deer's coat

as if trying to get inside, washes the antlers
of blood, like a curator cleaning the bones

of a saint in the crypt beneath a church
at the end of a century, when the people

have begun to think of the bodies
as truly dead and unraiseable,

when children have begun to carry knives
in their pockets. Once the last shred

of velvet falls to the ground, the deer
bends to eat it, nearly finished with ritual

and altar, the tree's side stripped of bark
while someplace in the world

a bomb strips away someone's skin.
The deer's mouth is stained with berries

of its own blood. Then, the deer is gone
and the tree left opened, the rain darkening

red against the hole in the sapwood.
The storm grows louder and louder

like a fear. The deer will shed
its velvet four more times before dying

of disease; the tree will grow its bark
again. Each atom in each cell will remember

the body it had made in this place, this time,
long after the rain flushes the river

to flood, long after this morning
when the country wakes to another war,

when two people wake in a house
and do not touch each other.

Beekeeping

It begins on the brightest
afternoon, my body

held in a corona

I can taste the sugar
and the heat of.

At the edge of the valley
wild hyacinths,

violet ones, scythe

through the shadows,
through my eye.

When I reach the hive
the bees cluster

on my veil like molecules

magnified, a code
to the core of things.

When I lift a comb

one bee stings my wrist,
then another,

the venom a note,

a pulse of light
that rises into a song:

a tower of spikes

or a swaying stalk
of purpling

blossoms. This must be
what love is:

a pain so radiant
it cuts through all others.

As the Sickle Moon Guts a Cloud

a sickness grows inside the moonlight,
turns under the mud in the corral
the horse churns to fever.
A boy stands at the fence
and whistles to the horse, clicks
his tongue, stamps his foot.
The horse will not come.
And when it does,
      when the boy offers it hay,
it bites the center of his palm
which purples with blood.
In twenty years, the boy
will place a shotgun in his mouth
      while his child sleeps.
Though they cannot be deciphered,
cannot become lighter,
all moments will shine
if you cut them open,
glisten like entrails in the sun.
      The fever grows deeper
into itself, tender-rooted flowers
inside the belly of the horse,
inside the eye of the boy
who again tries to feed it the hay,
gently cups its mouth.

Märchen

Lost in the forest one night, we find the body
of a wolf, its throat torn open,
the wound a cupful of rippling

black milk, where maggots curl star-white
in their glistening darkness.
The eyes hum with flies, which drone a joy

in the bones, the brain, wander
into the labyrinth through the tongue,
still hanging out in half-howl.

We keep walking, holding out our hands
to feel our way through the dark
as if we could touch as it touches,

know it as it knows the stars
that float in the vacuum of its voice,
that grow brighter and louder

until it unsays them, takes them
back. I know first there was light
to give the void a shape. I know

what has no beginning cannot end.
I can hardly see your face out here
but I can hear you breathing.

Your voice opens and says
I think the path is this way,
floats out, crosses to me

in a little cloud-boat and is gone—
Keep talking. How did the story go?
How dark it was inside the wolf,

which had begun as a clump
of darkness inside another wolf.
Then the child climbed out its belly

shining, without a name—
with only a red cap by which to call her
and the animal guts in her hands.

Lesson

After walking for many hours in the woods, I came
across a stag in a clearing,
      breathing inside the cold shine,
            a voice paused on a note.
As I approached, it leapt
and caught its antlers on the light's belly,
          spilling purple viscera
   everywhere. The stag broke
through bramble
      and stream, broke an owl-
call to pieces, broke further
     through the sun's remains,
       trampling the organs
into black blood as it ran.
The forest was dying
     around me. The leaves' last
       shadows punctured my face
as hooves did the ground,
     holes in the light's skin.
       I walked a little longer
before turning back home,
carrying in my shirt as many berries
as I could manage,
    my feet blistered from my boots,
     my arms bleeding from thorns.
Do you understand now?
Please, take and eat these. I'm sorry I hurt you.

Me Tangere

You follow me through the winter. The lake is already frozen
unconscious. When we walk the woods to gather kindling
you will not even touch my shoulder,

so exquisite is my form of grief, as if your hand would graze
away my skin. After dark, I walk out across the lake
      to feel the sky inhale.

I am cervine, a diamond smear, a single moment
of light gliding through fire-black trees,
as through a hole in time,
                until one night

I fall through the ice, and you find me in the grass afterward,
panting and kicking, my neck not fair but stained with mud

and blood from the jaws of that animal, and there it is written
in scar and sweat, in biting flies:
      Though I seem tame, I am wild to hold, so hold—

Rapture

Outside in the yard, our dogs are kicking snow
into specks of light,

like foals they tear through the marrow-
cloak of light, they break the light
in their mouths

            to warm their throats
as the snow rises around them,
as the snow pinpricks
the window of this room

like memory behind an eye and I
can feel the movement beginning,
the swell, the breaking

            into: the back door opening
and winter light opening wider
through the door
and the dogs running through it,

shaking it into the house, breathing
it into your palm, their scent

of cold and earth like bodies
too long in the ground,
they break the earth around us
            in their coming.

And then you bring your hand to your face,
your hand an invention of atoms
you brush across your forehead,

and then your hand
a sea boiling across
the back of my neck,

the forest there collapsing in a wave
and all the animals running
toward the edge to flee

the devastation:
a particle
that rises to float
                behind my eye—

View From the Fence, On Which
I Sit and Dangle My Legs

The horses are beating inside the field.
The horses are the night's blood

congealed. Moon-whipped horses,
frost-spun, clicking their teeth

against dead grass. Horses
with stomachs full of dust, how the flies

pick at their eyes, in love.
The horse lives in my eye without drowning.

Its ribs clatter like the train.
Horse with a broken leg,

with a bullet in your head, I saw you
in the stream last night.

You were eating the brain-star
fallen to the field. You

smelled of rifle-fire and cold.
I would make a violin, sing back,

but all the wood here burned.
The earth is burning, a funeral

after which nothing is buried.
Horse with the lash marks,

your one-eye filled with mine,
you search my palm for grain.

You shake the dust from your muscles
and it smells of spring.

The dust looks like a ghost
shattering. Then rain fallen across skin,

trickling from thigh to ankle,
down the back of the knee—

beauty, tickling the body
to laughter: I will follow you down.

Confession

I dream a pack of boys plays baseball in the road. They bat with an animal femur, and use a blackbird for a ball. All around them, bombs break the roofs of houses, break the cathedral glass and the cloud, break the shawled head of a woman, break the stone road apart, and the carriage horse's back. A boy swings and hits the ball, which is bleeding now, a mangled black lung wheezing through the air. When it reaches the sky, the blackbird breaks into many blackbirds. The blackbirds descend on the boys. Above, the war drones and swarms. No one can see me here. I hide under a thought of light, not incineration. The thought is a cloak I wake into gently: it is cold in the room, and I am hungry but whole. I open my eyes, climb out of bed. I pull a sweater over my head, fill the kettle. I break the hand, slice the heart—I mean I break the bread, slice the apple—and eat them.

Frühlingstraum

Dream of Spring

Barefoot in the yard, I tingle like a nape when touched.
All around, bees drag their dead from glittering hives.
    Here my mind knows its hold as a softness
of matter like a lake, and its thoughts as indentations
        on the lake, a near infinite rain.
I think of nothing. Then I think of coming days
I will spend with my knees in the grass,
or making love with the window open.
My hands feel weightless, upturned bodies in a deepening
            lake of sunlight.
What should I do with them?
    I kneel and push them into the ground,
dig a hole for a bulb. I scrape my palm on a rock
        and it bleeds into the soil
(which will bring tomatoes, strawberries). It is good
to be alive. Inside the house, I've fallen asleep sad
at the table again. I step through the backdoor
and go to wake myself. With my hand unwashed of dirt
and blood, I reach to touch the back of my neck.

The Last Przewalski's Horse

the last remaining species of wild horses

The bullet cleaves a jagged path
      through the tongue.
The bullet carves a glow
      in the skull, a black hole
in the brain, and the eyes
      roll up into the head.
The animal falls, a tangled,
      fly-bitten moon
the hunter kneels beside.
      He unsheathes his knife
and slices the breast-
      bone, up the abdomen,
then splits the pelvis, rolls
      organs from the opening:
little planets gone soft
      with blood. Cuts away
the glistening red web
      of matter around the heart
and rinses the cavity
      clean as, many years
from now, a flood will wash
      the valley of corpses.
One by one, he pulls
      each cuneiformed tooth
from the still-hot mouth,
      still smelling of grasses,
and plucks each hair
      from the tail for his violin.
Before dragging the body
      back to the house,

he ropes the legs together
        as if it could rise
from the dead.
        All night, the hunter
boils the bones.
        At dawn, he saws
open a radius, tongues out
        the jellied sunlight.
He cooks the brain into a stew
        that tastes of fog.
Sells the hide to a soldier,
        the teeth in a jar
to a curious boy, the curdling
        blood in bottles
to the wolf herder.
        Left the gristly heart
in the field. Left the eyes
        in the field, unable to close
and no use to anyone
        but the last flies of the season
which, a day before the snow
        finally kills them,
consume the retina
        piece by piece, photon
by photon, to see

The Dream of Water

Alone on a boat at night
with no wind. A magnetic field
glows inside each object, and each star
above pulls on my body,
and each fish in the sea turns

to ghost-trail, to concaved white.
The sea is a radiograph.
Then I touch the bones of my face.
They feel like water.
I see you standing on a far continent

and between us stretches
impenetrable darkness,
as if I must die to reach you.
I think the world
must be a hollow longing

filled with more of itself—
but no, darkness is a substance
that bends. I will oil and burn
my hands for light
before I stop searching.

Parable of the Flood

You know a flood is coming. The forest animals have fled.
The cattle, having broken the fence, are long gone.
Your hands float like the moons of two planets

orbiting a dead sun: cold islands gone numb.
You are watching the boatwright hammer nails into wood.
Watching the boatwright fasten a horsehide sail to a spine.

You just stand there, like a tongue without a mouth
to control it. The boatwright asks you to undress
and lie on the ground. He would like your skull

to light the way, your pulse to turn the engine blades,
your eye to focus the telescope lens. The boatwright
wants to break your throat into a luminous creaking.

You understand the boatwright as a figure of God.
You have no use for these things anymore.
Someone should cut out the stars' tongues, he says.

Someone should feed the moon's intestines to the dogs.
Standing in the field between forest and water, you want
to feel. Kneel, nod your head. Lay it against his blade.

When There Is Burning Instead

Isaiah 3:24

After the war, after they have torn the sinews
from the necks of sheep

in the countryside, the wolves
will come down from their forest

into the city, to eat the raw meat,
to lap blood from bone-bowls,

their paws against the roads
like the beat of a transplanted heart.

They will compass about me
where I lie. They will curiously graze

their teeth against my cheek
and lick the scrape on my hand

and I will not be afraid of them
because my blood is bitter

and my marrow rancid
and my skin is a linen of bees

and my tongue is split
into two songs, two branches

that grow soured figs
up through the charred

rubble of my throat. And I will sing
one into your mouth

if it would comfort you,
and I will sing the other

to comfort them,
though they will only hear me howling.

Purgatory

The deer walks the forest at night
and all the leaves bend to touch it.
It walks faster
and its hooves against dead leaves
rustle the sound of water.
                    Between its antlers a hole
deepens: an eye that remembers
nothing it has seen.
I shoot it, then cut away the meat,
which I must haul on my back
              till it rots,
but never eat. This is the task I must do
again and again as penance
              for a world destroyed.
But tonight, I linger: I saw
a femur in half to glimpse the glow
of the honeycomb
dripping through it, a relic
still warm
in the surrounding darkness,
              and the eye between my ribs
tears open—a memory beginning
again to beat. Love has been gone
for some time now.
I have sawed through my own leg
trying to find the way back.

Epilogue

Once children played war in the forest, prowled
    and leapt like wolves. Wind whipped snow through trees,
as if a ligament cut from the deer that a boy
    thought of devouring, though he told no one.
A girl pretended to scalp a boy and a boy smeared
    sap on the wound of another and one girl hid
in a branch like the owl that once perched there.
    Once deer slept in the forest. Once the forest
had the greenest leaves. Once it felt silence.
    Once, the weight of soldiers. In the forest
broken fog hovers, the rotting blossoms of clouds.
    Late in the forest, the snow patches darken:
love's bloody tufts of fur, strewn across the ground.
    Loneliness, that lioness, licks what's left.
On cold nights, the children used to pull their knees
    up to their chests, little bone piles in their beds.
In one story, a fox curled into a tree hollow
    like a flame into a corpse's mouth. And in another
the children woke. They put on their boots.

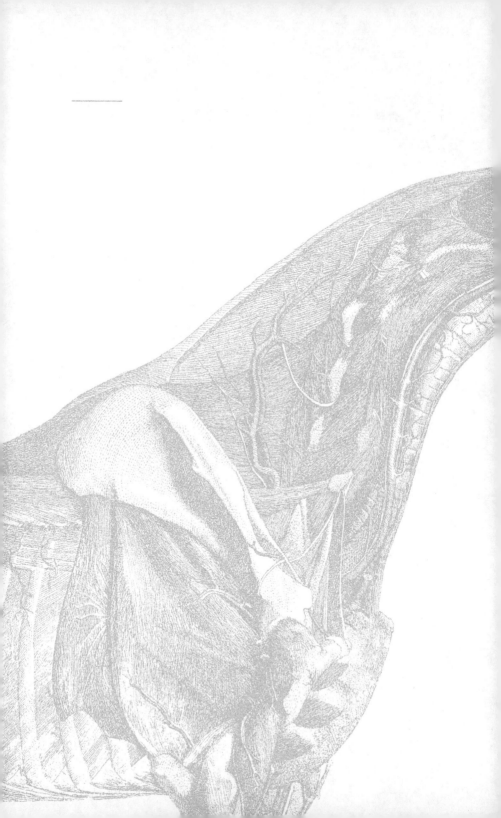

Pathfinder

Primordial Sea

Black noon. A black wind
wrinkles the fields.

Night flowers open
like white gills to breathe.

Moonlight slivers my eye,
silvers my neck

which you open gently
to lick my oozing light.

We've become blind
and bioluminescent.

Our words part
the water into paths.

As we roam the lush
weeds of darkness

our eyes grow
backward into our heads

and Lord, I can see far
inside you then.

Primeval Forest

Here, the mind must grow into itself.
You are the thought
of the animal. Or the animal
of the thought,
walking on all fours through pines.
You, the thought of a word
in a shadow tongue.

Open your mouth—you animal,
not yet machine—and say
anything, speak your way home;
devour the violets,
electrify your throat,
your new-grown tongue with violets.

Prison

Find a path through it:

Think: a blizzard of clover,
a wildfire of foxes
pawing at the door.

Recall a name:
a pocketwatch
unwound to stone

in your hand
so you can hold it for as long
as you need.

Think the prison
into a garden,

your shadow
into a basket to gather
all the apples.

Think, prisoner:
a forest, a city
unsheathed:

think the floodwater
rolling back
all the bodies

that once covered the mouth
of the valley—

your mouth—
and all the bees fly out
and all the pollen
and all the sun.

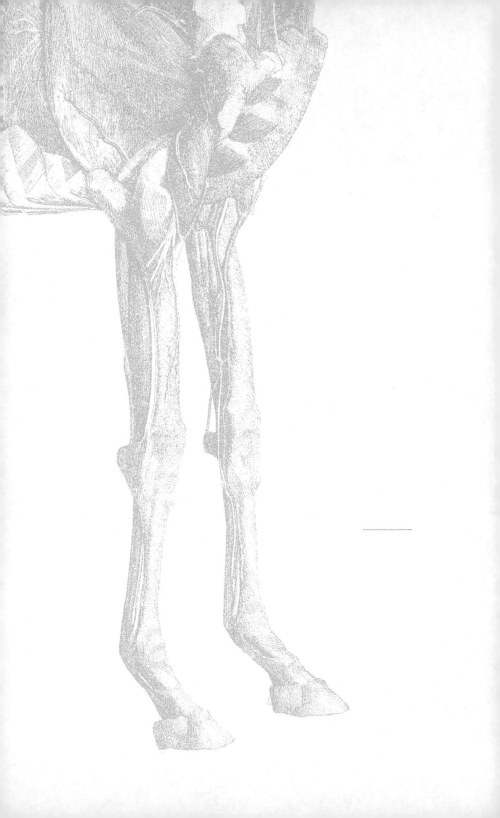

Sea Psalm

Frail is our vessel, and the ocean is wide
ST. AUGUSTINE

Lord, this is not your world. I am not yours
but also not mine. Not your passenger.
Not your saint at the helm, the machinery

of my hands turning like clocks.
Not your reliquary. Not your daughter
in oilskins, hauling up the iron cross

to follow the directional light. Water slinks
wolfish in my wake, foam gathering
like shorn light—the hours pulled under.

Look there: a fish flails on the deck, halved
into a scaled book, its milk and blood
spilled for cockroaches and birds. Look

down: my chest is opened, the wind plucks
its thin, blue notes. Soon this ocean
will rise, will come pouring into my ears,

my throat, will tear the bones from my hands
and the boneless fish of this tongue
from my mouth. Lord, when my blood

reaches the city, it will be the water
of the river they bring to their mouths
and the name they thank will be yours.

Question

Body my crossing   my horse
body my season of visions
body my cauldron   the dark churning
of the water inside
        body my harpoon   my hook
in the mouth of the world
body the frost floats out your mouth
like a dream   body your fallen light
the sunken sound of your voice
in the water   body your well
carrying skulls of the dead
body your open gate
                letting the horse outside
the clouds like a dream
        lowering into the mouth
of the world   I am crossing
        the season of water
I am trying to unhook my hand from the dream
I am trying to find the breach
but there is no end to your widening
body where is your latch   the moment
        you touch a body

Elegy Surrounded by Water

Out at sea, each night
is long. Each night

has one sound I know:
the moon against the water

like your cheek across mine
in another life.

I am finding a way
to reach where you are.

I am thinking of lighting
the voice on fire.

Of lighting the dark oil
of the sea on fire,

each drop a note
singing the daylight up.

Listen—I am
trying to send you

a human sound,
which is bones

cracking to bend an arrow
back, a long whistle

across the field
of a body you remember

because it remembers
yours. We are built

to live in each other.
This means we are built

to ruin. Each night
I dream back another piece

of you—an eye,
a ligament—and each day

wake on the water
with another hole.

Archipelago: Island of Sheep

after The Voyage of Saint Brendan

First: darkness and nothing.
Then, a swell of darkness,

my hands so small inside it.
Ahead, I see the sheep,

tiny cathedrals
glowing on the island.

They walk their night
like a blindness,

their island an eye
plucked from its socket,

and its pasture
the way earth tries to see

in the world of water.
These are the lambs

that shepherds once carried
across their necks.

They wait here, listening
for their return—

for they know
their masters' voices—

and so when I step
they do not come

nor scatter; they hover,
little clouds,

motes in the eye
that cannot assemble me.

I lay down—
I lay among them

and slept like a shadow
as you sleep in the night

of my skull, among
the soft-bright bodies

long dead, and the whirring
black flowers.

Archipelago: The Paradise of Birds

How can an incorporeal light burn
corporeally in a corporeal creature?
THE VOYAGE OF SAINT BRENDAN

I come to a series of lights in the fog.
The lights fly in a halo over an island.
One light lands on the mast, cleans soot

from its feathers: a simple bird.
Nearer, they seem stars crafted in a furnace:
loaves for a hand to break,

as my god broke me. If you could see
how these miracles drag my eye
through the fog, singing *We endure*

no suffering, you would understand
why I anchor, notch an arrow
and step into them, braced to ignite.

Archipelago: Tabula Rasa

As foretold, all the island
is made of brightness:

a curved honeycomb,
a feverish brain

cast from its skull.
I've come for cleansing.

The bees crawl into my ears
to begin their work.

They burn inside me
like many stars,

and all the tiny tombs
inside me open,

and each chamber
is lit clean, shaking

with the island's word-
less reverberation.

The bees leave one
honey-bead on the roof

of my mouth:
a thought

that erases you
from me. Each atom

begins again.
Except for this one,

this black speck
still in my eye,

like your pupil
in the sunlight

in the last room
you entered:

I remember.
You saw me.

Archipelago: The Soporific Well

Some of them drank one cup, others two, and the rest
three. The last were overcome by a sleep of three days
and three nights.

THE VOYAGE OF SAINT BRENDAN

After days of thirst, the island appears as hands bringing the sea up
     to a mouth, its leaves like drops of water across a palm.
I step from my boat onto its shore, walk through the trees
     for hours, looking for a creek, deer tracks, any sign
of life. I reach a well cradled by roots and stones. Inside
     sits a brightness of milk, like a muted word.
I drink three handfuls, open my eyes in a field of terrible white.
     There is a well in the center, and inside it a darkness
with no reflection. I think: lost sound with no one to hear it,
     sound of the dead, your voice, which is like the moment
a star closes its wave of light, which is like my body
     curled on the ground. Where I wake. My head opens
its eyes, terrified the rest of its body rots in the well. Three days
     bloom a purple garden in my mouth. No animal comes to eat
the constellation of blossoms, this waking the distant expansion
     of a universe that cannot feel us.

Instructions for Wintering on the Ice Field

Work your hands often
or they will swell purple
and turn feral
and flee from your wrists.
Unhook your body
from its fear of this vastness,
this dream of the sea
where clouds shift
their bone map,
erase your footsteps
again and again.
Here, where the land
is a form of water,
all freezes to light.
Even you.
But you will thaw
and part your skin
for a single, black tendril.
It will grow
as if through stone
in the ruins
of your beloved city
centuries after it has fallen.

Letter from the Ice Field, October

The dream was bright, but small.
My body was inside out,
a sick elegy to its beauty.
I walked until I found a single tree.
You were picking its apples
in the straw-light in a straw hat,
handed me one without spots.
Put this where your heart rots, you said
and I did, I was happy.
When I woke, the ice
was rocking, unaware, a cold
breathing cast from a body—
You gave much.
Thank you for
the last good thing.

Letter from the Ice Field, December

In the dream, you stand at the end
of the field beyond the house.

You bury something.
Your hands glow like milk in the dark.

You bend, your shovel lifts pieces
of moonlight into the air.

I try to call you inside
but my mouth locks with frost.

The room of the skull floods with snow.
I have forgotten how you sound.

Your hands fall like milk
into the well of darkness you dig

and I cannot see beyond it.
This is to say, I wake

with a deeper void. I am beginning
to see the body as a well

and your absence as a thirst
that pushes its hands

down my throat, lifts the bucket,
drinks and drinks. A saint said

when the dead visit us in dreams
they cannot know what they do.

You came to the field.
You cut off your ears.

Your hands fell through me—
two lights I almost broke

in half wanting. Tell me
what you thought you were doing

when you tried to lay your body
into that ground.

Letter from the Ice Field, January

Again I rode through the forest of dead trees. I rode through the swamp of blood, alone, thinking nothing of you or anyone. I rode until I found the remains of the town in a clearing, where I stopped, and walked down into the crypt, knowing a saint had lain there for centuries. Her mouth lay open, as if to ferry over the word of a messenger. The saint had my face. The saint woke and rose from her coffin, and gave me her skin, which is a map of the earth, and her eyes, which see every planet. I took out my eyes and put hers in, then climbed into her empty coffin, my body glowing as hers had: like a femur in a fire, its marrow burning across the length of me. The burning was the sound of your voice, I remember—calling me across the lake that winter—*Come over to this side, I found some dry wood*—and look, you have found me again. Inside me you have learned to speak impossibly.

Letter from the Ice Field, March

It is so cold I cannot feel my body.
When wind sharpens

       and slides
       its steel through my ear

a quake shifts inside me
like liquid

       in the compass
       I dropped into the sea.

I am afraid to fall that way,
as a weight

       from a hand
       into some bottomless

country of water.
Once, I hoped we became

       more than an aperture.
       Once God

was my anchor
in the nickering sea.

       Love was mine
       in the falling one.

I dream I walk a forest
until I reach, again,

        the stone house
        with a moss floor.

A vine of sunlight
grows at its center.

Where you would have been standing.
Where I am parted.

Archipelago: Ultima Thule

island farthest north, in perpetual daylight

Terrible continent no one has ridden,
I come from a country near ruin,

    from a forest lit only by rifle fire,

 where leaves are torn tongues
grown from plucked-out eyes,

    where a boy, fallen from a tree,

lies bleeding for the wolves,
 where men kill and then wash

    the blood from their hands

 into the rivers. I drank that water
and washed my feet in it.

    Here I rinse my face in this light,

 drink this snow, a primordial moment
I cup in my hands, now so cold

    they've begun to blacken

from frost. The bones of the island
moan as I walk across them,

    opening malignant flowers

of sound across the ground.
Wind deepens the wounds

    I leave with my boots. Nothing

is well. Even death's bones
have broken so many times

    they have no symmetry, but still

death is dutiful, I will be dutiful—
I will excavate the artifact,

    sift shadows from the shadowless.

 And I'll be true to my love
if my love is not true to me.

The City Where Men Are Mended

After years riding in the wilderness
I come to the city
after a war has ended.

It is the middle of the night.
The city breathes
like my horse out of breath

against my thighs.
All the soldiers
are dead or wounded.

Inside the hospital
nurses unravel bandages
from their eyes

to clean them, so the city
tastes of blood
meeting water in a basin.

A silence has eaten
through the city
like a flood through a cathedral—

the kind of devotion
that scours a building's bones
to nothing.

I have been silent
for very long, having no god.
Violent, unmerciful.

When I came to the city
my tongue rode up my throat:
an outlaw come back,

carrying in a satchel
a bloody heart, the truth
I would tell a man.

Any one of them.
If he had ears.
Could walk to the door.

Let Us Consider Where We Might Have a Home

—THE SEAFARER

Wildflowers have begun to grow again
at the bottom of the mountain

where two boys once stood together,
watching the elk graze, and the clouds.

The boys picked some of the flowers
for their mother. The road they walked

curls back into the mouth of the town,
as if unsaying it. Consider the radio

still crackling a warning throughout
the house, and the residue of a glow

that dusts the wildflowers in their vase,
and the faint smell of burnt skin.

Consider the bees come to dwell
in the roof of the rotted-out

barn, humming like the man
who used to feed the horses there, bled

the cow while the boys watched
before they left to wander the hills

to collect the wildflowers.
Consider such empty afternoons.

Cut the rot from the apple you find.
Mend the hole in your coat.

Tend a tomato plant up and up
and share its fruit with the foxes.

But first, you must
build a coffin for the remains here.

Find the hammer in the toolbox
and pull the delicately rusted nails

from the eyes in the wood plank.
Before lashing the axe you've found

against the black-blistered tree,
walk back to the house, through the garden

of skeletons, to get the sutures
and gauze from the medicine cabinet—

you will need to use them
before the hardest work is done.

How the World Was Made

And I saw the anatomy of the word, the anatomy
of the sleeping eye, of the bleeding star
at the edge of implosion. Of the mouth as it prays
against another mouth. Of the mouth remade
into the smallest island of finches. Anatomy of the sea
before the land fractured it. Anatomy
of the ancient ferns, the reptilian eye of the dark form
hovering between them. Anatomy of adagio
and of the voice. Anatomy of the prayer
between mouths, of the space between words
in the book laid under the tongue. Anatomy of histories,
of each other world entwining with this one—
a diagram of light and dark matter stretched
across the surface. Everything was veined, everything
given shape and bone and muscle to fill it.
Everything became mortal but I could hold it.
I could hold it, and it held me. I heard each thing stir
awake. And I knew the answer. Take this
throat, its slender tangle. Then breathe into it.

Equinox

In the pasture by my house, the snow melts
to paths of not-quite-light, like a map
for sun to follow.
        The horses there are unkempt,
obscured by pink blots of mange.
They walk all morning, catching flies in their ribs,
twitching like restless, half-wild minds.
I know their teeth could sever my fingers.
I know their hooves
        could break through my chest.
I know the inscription of their breath
is an invisible benediction.
        Today, I'll groom those animals,
though they aren't mine.
Tomorrow I'll plant a garden
and in four months bring them carrots.
Soon the whitest sky will shatter, haphazardly
        plant its crystal in our skin.
Then the dead will walk.
And I will come by your house, carrying
bread, eggs, apples. Milk colder than moon.

NOTES

"Me Tangere" is a response to "Whoso List to Hunt" by Sir Thomas Wyatt. The title and the line "'Though I seem tame, I am wild to hold, so hold—" are reimaginings of the final couplet: "Noli me tangere; for Cæsar's I am, / And wild for to hold, though I seem tame."

"Pathfinder" is titled after a passage from Marina Tsvetaeva's essay "Pushkin and Pugachev":

> There are magical words, magical apart from their meanings, physically magical, with a magic inherent in the sound itself, words that before they deliver a message already have a meaning, words that are signs and meanings unto themselves, that do not require comprehension, but only hearing, words of the animals, the child's dream language. It is possible that each person has in his own life his own magic words. In my life, the magic word was and remains – the Pathfinder.

"Question" is in conversation with May Swenson's poem of the same title.

The Island of Sheep, The Paradise of Birds, and The Soporific Well are islands Saint Brendan is said to have visited during his voyage to find the Isle of the Blessed in the sixth century. The epigraphs that begin "The Paradise of Birds" and "The Soporific Well" come from *The Voyage of Saint Brendan (Navigatio sancti Brendani abbatis)*, translated by John Joseph O'Meara.

The lines "And I'll be true to my love / if my love is not true to me" are a variation of the lyric "I'll be true to my love / if my love will be true to me" from the traditional folk ballad "Two Sisters."

The title "The City Where Men Are Mended" is borrowed from the first line of "The Stones" by Sylvia Plath.

ACKNOWLEDGEMENTS

To the editors and staff of the journals in which these poems, or different versions of them, first appeared, you have my thanks:

Best New Poets 2009: "How the World Was Made"

Boston Review: "Letter from the Ice Field, December"

Connotation Press: An Online Artifact: "Fable," "The Last Przewalski's Horse," "Archipelago: Island of Sheep," "Archipelago: Paradise of Birds, "Archipelago: Ultima Thule"

Crab Orchard Review: "Deer Rub"

Memorious: "Question," "The Dream of Water"

Meridian: "Epilogue"

New England Review: "View from the Fence, on Which I Sit and Dangle My Legs"

Ninth Letter: "Rapture"

Pleiades: "Confession," "Märchen," "Purgatory," "When There Is Burning Instead"

Southern Indiana Review: "Sea Psalm," "Archipelago: Tabula Rasa"

Sugar House Review: "Frühlingstraum," "Instructions for Wintering on the Ice Field," "Letter from the Ice Field, October"

TriQuarterly: "As the Sickle Moon Guts a Cloud," "Parable of the Flood"

Vinyl Poetry: "Archipelago: The Soporific Well," "Elegy Surrounded by Water"

"Question," "Letter from the Ice Field, December" and "How the World Was Made" were featured in the anthology *Read Women*, published by Locked Horn Press in 2014.

My deepest gratitude to the National Poetry Series and everyone at Milkweed Editions, and to the Rona Jaffe Foundation and the Fine Arts Work Center in Provincetown, without whose support this book would not have been possible.

Sincere gratitude, also, to all my teachers for the generosity of their instruction and dedication, especially Lyrae Van Clief-Stefanon, Geri Doran, Garrett Hongo, Jacqueline Osherow, Paisley Rekdal, Katharine Coles, Sean Serrell, and Rita Green.

Thank you to Martha Collins, Marianne Boruch, and Brigit Pegeen Kelly for their guidance on this book, or portions of it, as well as for their encouragement and kindness during that process.

Thank you to Bread Loaf Writers' Conference for the opportunity to workshop material from this book at a crucial stage in its development.

And thank you to all my colleagues at Cornell University, the University of Oregon, and the University of Utah, and to everyone else for their friendships and feedback: Rebecca Lindenberg, Margaret Reges, Susannah Nevison, Laura Bylenok, Claire Wahmanholm, Nikki Zielinski, Thomas Watson, and Corey Van Landingham. And to my parents and Steve: thank you, always, for your unwavering faith in me.

SARA ELIZA JOHNSON has received numerous honors, including a Rona Jaffe Foundation Writers' Award, a fellowship from the Fine Arts Work Center in Provincetown, and a scholarship to the Bread Loaf Writers' Conference. Her poetry has appeared in *Boston Review*, *Pleiades*, *Ninth Letter*, and the *Best New Poets* series, among others. She is currently a doctoral student at the University of Utah, where she is the Vice Presidential Fellow in creative writing. She lives in Salt Lake City.

Interior design & typesetting by Mary Austin Speaker

Typeset in Walbaum. Walbaum is a Modern Didone typeface
designed at the turn of the nineteenth century in the German city of
Weimar by Justus Erich Walbaum, and cut for machine composition
by the Monotype corporation in the late 1930s.

milkweed
editions

Founded as a nonprofit organization in 1980, Milkweed Editions is an independent publisher. Our mission is to identify, nurture and publish transformative literature, and build an engaged community around it.

milkweed.org